The Air Fryer Cookbook
The Complete Guide

30 Top Healthy And
Delicious Recipes

Mia Kendal

is not engaging in the rendering of legal, financial, medical or professional advice.

By reading this document, the reader agrees that under no circumstances are we responsible for any losses, direct or indirect, which are incurred as a result of the use of information contained within this document, including, but not limited to, —errors, omissions, or inaccuracies.

Contents

Introduction

Naturally, you are obviously very excited right now to open up the packaging of your shiny new device and start creating your next culinary masterpiece using your Air Fryer!

But wait! Let me stop you right there for a moment.

Going into exploring the Air Fryer on your own might be a bad idea as you might end up making a mess of yourself, which will ultimately lead to disappointment.

And that is exactly why I have included this introductory chapter! To save you from the risk of going under the bus while trying to work with your new, gorgeous appliance!

Always keep in mind that it is of utmost importance to have a very good understanding of the appliance that you are using in order to be able to unlock its full potential and utilize it properly so that you can create your dream meals.

So, without any further delays, let's start with the most basic of all questions.

What is an Air Fryer?

By now you have most probably seen a number of different advertisements trying to explain how "an Air Fryer is a wonderful device that seamlessly utilizes hot air to cook food"!

But let me tell one thing, there is a little more to an Air Fryer than simply that.

An Air Fryer device is a fantastic, modern piece of kitchen equipment that not only helps to make one's life easier, but also elevates your lifestyle by providing you with a healthier food palate that minimizes the use of oil.

In fact, the popularity of oil free cooking and the Air Fryer device has reached such high levels that Gordon Ramsey himself claimed that "Air is the new oil".

An in-depth look at the cooking mechanism

Now that you have your device in your hand, you must be wondering, "What makes this so special?"

The answer lies predominantly within the way it prepares meals. While most of the cooking appliances out there rely on conventional methods of conduction heat, the Air Fryer does a phenomenal job in going against the common trend by utilizing a method of convection heating.

The "Air" here is what is responsible for the magic that happens. Back then when this technology was first introduced to the mass market, it was met with massive acclaim and still to this day, this method of cooking doesn't fail to impress chefs around the world.

During your journey around the various supermarkets looking for an Air Fryer, you have most definitely seen the word "Rapid Air Technology" countless times. That actually refers to a very delicately designed process which the Air Fryer uses to cook its food.

Upon sucking up the air into its intake chamber, the appliance immediately cranks up the heat and raises the temperature of the air to about 200°C. The air is then passed on to a highly specialized cooking cell where the meal is prepared and cooked. This whole process is the mechanism behind the term "Rapid Air Technology".

One of the biggest benefits this has is that thanks to the use of "Air", the device pretty much diminishes the quantity of oil needed in preparing meals. This helps to promote a new and improved healthier lifestyle which encourages you to try out everything from grilling, frying and even baking.

And the best part of it all? You can do all of these without using an excess amount of oil!

The different components of a fryer

For absolute newcomers, the various parts of an Air Fryer might seem a little bit confusing. Don't be alarmed as they are pretty easy to master once you discover the roles of each of the parts.

- **The Cooking Chamber:** This is the place where the magic happens and the food actually gets cooked. The functionality here varies a little bit depending on which branded fryer you are using, in the sense that the cooking chamber might have the capacity of holding just a single tray or a multi layered tray.

- **Heating Element:** The heating element is responsible for the level of heat which needs to be transferred to the passing air. A very desirable feature with most Air Fryers is that whenever it reaches the specified temperature for cooking, the heating element automatically turns itself off to save power and prevent further overheating.

- **Fan and Grill:** The fan and the grill tend to work in conjunction with each other in order to ensure that the superheated air is evenly distributed around your food. The mechanical design of the grill allows it to adjust the direction of the air flow, which plays a large part in the whole cooking process.

- **Exhaust System:** The exhaust system in this appliance is designed to help maintain a stable internal pressure and prevent buildup of harmful air. Some models add a filter which clears out the dust and other left over particles to clean out the exhausted air, making sure that it does not release any unpleasant odors.

- **Transferable Food Tray:** This is basically the tray where you are going to place the food that you want to cook. There are some brands out there that give you the added advantage of having several boundary walls built within the tray itself which allows you cook dishes of several different types at once. Other than that, some brands might even provide a universal handle, so you will be able to pull out your tray from the heating chamber with ease.

The Very Basic Features of Your Fryer

While the different brands out there are sure to add a little flavor of their own, the following features are common to almost all the Air Fryers on the market.

- **Automated Temperature Control System:** This is one of the more crucial and essential elements of an Air Fryer which plays a significant role in determining how the final product turns out to be.
  The automatic temperature control system allows the appliance to keep track of the temperature and turn off the system when the airflow reaches a specific temperature. This allows each and every meal to be created according to the user's personal preferences.
- **Digital Screen and Touch Panel:** We are living in a generation where each and every individual has a touch enabled smart phone! We have invariably habituated ourselves to using them.

The manufacturers of the Air Fryer are fully aware of this fact and to make their devices more accessible, they have implemented full touch screens on their devices. This greatly helps newcomers to easily acquaint themselves with the new appliance and start cooking right away using the pre-set heat settings and other functionalities.

- **A Convenient Buzzer:** This is a feature that is included in Air Fryers to make the cooking experience much easier for those individuals who are more inclined towards the lazier side of life. However, staring at the Air Fryer until the meal is done might actually be a test of patience for some people. The buzzer and timer of Air Fryers allow individuals to know when their dish is ready, thanks to the buzzing sound which the device makes when the timer runs out.

- **An Assorted Selection of Cooking Presets:** Not all of us are born maestros when it comes to cooking. Some of us just want to eat whatever we can find time. The Air Fryer comes fully packed with a wide selection of pre-set timings for any number of meals, which makes it much easier for anyone who is inexperienced in cooking. They don't have to worry about figuring out the timing for the perfect dish as it is already pre-set for their convenience.

PRESET BUTTON COOKING CHART		
PRESET BUTTON	TEMPERATURE	TIME
French Fries	400°F	20 min
Roasts	370°F	15 min
Shrimp	330°F	15 min
Baked Goods	350°F	25 min
Chicken	380°F	25 min
Steak	380°F	25 min
Fish	390°F	25 min

Advantages of owning an Air Fryer

Aside from the fact that using an Air Fryer cuts down your oil usage by about 80%, there are some other advantages which you might want to consider before buying/while using your Air Fryer to make you feel more confident.

- Air Fryers are very easy to use and are very user friendly.
- Cleaning the fryer is extremely easy.
- Since the meals produced utilize very minimal amounts of oil, the meals also contribute to weight loss.
- The fryer allows for very rapid cooking that saves a whole lot of your daily time.

Simple steps to use your Air Fryer

Now, obviously the cooking procedure will vary from one meal to the next, but the core steps will remain largely the same when it comes to cooking using an Air Fryer. In general, the steps are:

- Firstly, before beginning the preparation of any of your meals, you should gently take out the cooking basket and drizzle it with just a little bit of oil.
- Take the ingredients of your meal and put them in the drizzled tray. However, this might vary a little bit depending on your meal. For example, if you are going to be baking a cake, then you might want to put your batter in a separate dish first, and then place the dish inside the cooking tray.
- Set the temperature to your specified level and depending on your meal, set up the timer as well.

- Some meals might require you to shake up the basket from time to time. This will be noted in the "How To" section of the recipes.
- And just like that, your food should be ready.

However, as an added bonus, I am going to include a brief list of some of the more common standard meals which you might be interested in preparing before diving into the complicated ones.

➢ **Thick Frozen Fries**

Min Amount: 11oz.
Maximum Amount: 43oz
Time Taken: 12 – 22 minutes
Temperature: 360 °F
Halfway Shake Needed: Yes
Extra Remarks: Nil

➢ **Thin Frozen Fries**

Min Amount: 11oz.
Maximum Amount: 43oz.
Time Taken: 9 – 19 minutes
Temperature: 360 °F
Halfway Shake Needed: Yes
Extra Remarks: Nil

➢ **Homemade Fries**

Min Amount: 11oz. / 21oz.
Maximum Amount: 32oz. /43oz.
Time Taken: 15 – 22 minutes / 18 – 25 minutes
Temperature: 360 °F
Halfway Shake Needed: Yes
Extra Remarks: You will need to soak the fries for 30 minutes in ¼ tablespoon of oil for 11oz.; 3/4 tablespoon for 32oz.; ½ tablespoon for 21oz. and 1 tablespoon for 43oz.

➢ **Potato Wedges**

Min Amount: 11oz. / 21oz.
Maximum Amount: 32oz.
Time Taken: 18 – 21 minutes / 24 minutes
Temperature: 360 °F
Halfway Shake Needed: Yes
Extra Remarks: You will need to soak the fries for 30 minutes in ¼ tablespoon of oil for 11oz.; 3/4 tablespoon for 32oz.; ½ tablespoon for 21oz.

➢ **Potato Cubes**

Min Amount: 11oz. / 21oz.
Maximum Amount: 32oz.
Time Taken: 18 – 21 minutes / 24 minutes
Temperature: 360 °F
Halfway Shake Needed: Yes
Extra Remarks: You will need to soak the fries for 30 minutes in ¼ tablespoon of oil for 11oz.; 3/4 tablespoon for 32oz.; ½ tablespoon for 21oz.

➢ **Cheese Sticks**

Min Amount: 4oz.
Maximum Amount: 16oz.
Time Taken: 8 - 10 minutes
Temperature: 360 °F
Halfway Shake Needed: Yes
Extra Remarks: Nil

➢ **Cheese Sticks**

Min Amount: 11oz.
Maximum Amount: 43oz.
Time Taken: 9 – 19 minutes
Temperature: 360 °F
Halfway Shake Needed: Yes
Extra Remarks: Preferable to use oven ready version

➢ **Chicken Nuggets**

Min Amount: 1oz.
Maximum Amount: 14.
Time Taken: 6 minutes
Temperature: 330/390 °F
Halfway Shake Needed: Yes
Extra Remarks: Preferable to use oven ready version

➢ **Fish Sticks**

Min Amount: 4oz.

Maximum Amount: 12oz.
Time Taken: 8 – 10 minutes
Temperature: 390 °F
Halfway Shake Needed: No
Extra Remarks: Preferable to use oven ready version

> **Steak**

Min Amount: 4oz.
Maximum Amount: 21oz.
Time Taken:
For 4 oz. – you should cook it for 5 minutes at 360 degrees Fahrenheit, followed by 4 minutes at 150 degrees Fahrenheit
For 21 oz. – you should cook it for 6 minutes at 360 degrees Fahrenheit, followed by 4 minutes at 150 degrees Fahrenheit
Temperature: 360 °F
Halfway Shake Needed: No
Extra Remarks: Nil

> **Hamburger**

Min Amount: 4oz.
Maximum Amount: 14oz.
Time Taken: 6/7 minutes
Temperature: 360 °F
Halfway Shake Needed: No
Extra Remarks: Nil

> **Chicken Wings**

Min Amount: 3oz.
Maximum Amount: 21oz.
Time Taken: 18 to 22 minutes
Temperature: 360 °F
Halfway Shake Needed: No
Extra Remarks: Nil

➢ **Chicken Breast**

Min Amount: 3oz.
Maximum Amount: 21oz.
Time Taken:
For 4 oz. – you should cook it for 8 minutes at 290 degrees Fahrenheit, followed by 6 minutes at 360 degrees Fahrenheit
For 21 oz. – you should cook It for 8 minutes at 290 degrees Fahrenheit, followed by 8 minutes at 360 degrees Fahrenheit
Temperature: 360 °F
Halfway Shake Needed: No
Extra Remarks: Nil

➢ **Cake**

Min Amount: 1oz.
Maximum Amount: 24oz.
Time Taken: 30 minutes
Temperature: 320 °F
Halfway Shake Needed: No

Extra Remarks: Nil

How to clean your Air Fryer easily

- Remove the power cable from the wall and make sure that the device is completely cooled.
- Wipe out the external part of the fryer using a moist cloth dipped in mild detergent.
- Clean the outer basket and the fryer basket using hot water mixed with mild detergent and a soft sponge.
- Clean the inner part of the appliance using hot water with mild detergent and a soft sponge.
- If you find that some residue is stuck in the heating element, use a cleaning brush to clear it out.

Some extra tips

- If you find any sticky food residue in the cooking basket, clean the basket with a little bit of dish detergent.
- To ensure that the basket is cleaned well, if possible, soak your cooking basket under dish detergent water for a few minutes and rinse it thoroughly under hot water.
- Try to avoid using metal utensils and cleaning brushes while cleaning your appliance as it might scratch the body of your fryer.

Some mistakes to avoid

- Always make sure that you keep your Air Fryer in an area where it gets enough air flow.
- When you are not using the device, make sure to turn off the device completely.
- The fryer heats up very quickly, so there is no need to pre-heat your fryer way ahead of time. Just pre-heat it immediately before cooking.
- Make sure to thaw your food before placing it into your fryer basket to make sure that it is thoroughly cooked.

How to deal with some common problems

- Not working properly: Make sure that your device is properly plugged in and the preparation time and temperature are set.
- Food not cooked properly: If this problem occurs, then try to cook your meals in smaller batches. If that fails as well, increase the temperature a bit.
- Food not evenly fried: Some meals require you to shake the fryer basket from time to time, so keep that in mind.
- White smoke emitted from fryer: This happens if you have used too much oil.
- Basket not sliding in properly: This might sometimes happen if you have overfilled your basket. Make sure to not exceed the maximum specified limit of your basket.

With all of that said, you are now ready to dive into the recipes and start your Air Fryer journey!

Chapter 1: Breakfast Recipes

A Fine Berryful French Breakfast

Serving: 2

Prep Time: 5 minutes

Cook Time: 10 minutes

Ingredients

- ➢ 2 large eggs
- ➢ 1 teaspoon of vanilla extract
- ➢ 2 thick slices of sourdough bread
- ➢ Bread butter for spreading mixed berries
- ➢ Squeeze of honey
- ➢ Low-fat plain Greek yoghurt

How To

- ➢ Pre-heat the Air Fryer to a temperature of 356 ° F.
- ➢ Take a bowl and beat the eggs
- ➢ Mix in the vanilla
- ➢ Take a piece of bread and gently butter both sides of it
- ➢ Soak the bread in egg and mix it until the egg has been fully absorbed
- ➢ Take out the frying basket and gently place the bread on top of the basket
- ➢ Let it cook for about 6 minutes, making sure that you turn it halfway
- ➢ Once done, serve with mixed berries, honey and yoghurt

Nutrition Values (Per Serving)

- Fat: 57g
- Protein: 11g
- Dietary Fiber: 2.4g
- Calories: 240.2

Perfectly Blended Turkey And Ham Sandwich

Serving: 4

Prep Time: 5 minutes

Cook Time: 10 minutes

Ingredients

- 8 slices whole wheat bread
- 4 slices lean turkey ham
- 4 slices cheese
- 8 slices tomato

How To

- ➤ Top each piece of bread with cheese, tomato and turkey ham
- ➤ Cover them with the remaining bread
- ➤ Heat your fryer to 360 °F
- ➤ Place the sandwich inside your fryer and cook for about 10 minutes until the bread is a nice golden brown color
- ➤ Serve hot

Nutrition Values (Per Serving)

- Calories: 294
- Carbohydrate: 25g
- Protein: 16g
- Fat: 15g

Mini Zucchini With Feta Quiche

Serving: 4

Prep Time: 10 minutes

Cook Time: 40 minutes

<u>**Ingredients**</u>

- 12 ounces thawed puff pastry
- 4 large eggs
- ¼ cup milk
- 1 medium sized thinly sliced zucchini
- 4 oz. drained and crumbled feta cheese
- 2 tablespoons of chopped fresh dill
- Olive oil spray
- Kosher salt as needed
- Freshly ground black pepper

<u>**How To**</u>

- ➢ Pre-heat the Air Fryer to 360° F
- ➢ Whisk together eggs and season them with pepper and salt
- ➢ Add the zucchini, dill and feta cheese
- ➢ Stir well
- ➢ Lightly grease 8 individual muffin tins
- ➢ Roll out your pastry and cover the bottom and sides of your mini pie tins
- ➢ Divide the egg mix and pour them into your prepared tins
- ➢ Cook them in batches, each batch for 15-20 minutes until the crusts show a fine golden texture
- ➢ Transfer them to a serving dish and enjoy!

<u>**Nutrition Values (Per Serving)**</u>

- Calories: 201
- Carbohydrate: 13g
- Protein: 11g
- Fat: 12g

A Good Morning Wonton Delight

Serving: 2

Prep Time: 10 minutes

Cook Time: 24 minutes

Ingredients

- 10 wanton wrappers
- 150 g prawns
- 1 can crab meat
- 3 thinly sliced spring onions
- 6 oz. melted butter
- 1 tablespoon of grated fresh ginger
- 1 minced garlic clove
- 1 tablespoon of olive oil
- Sweet and sour sauce

How To

- ➢ Shred the peeled potatoes, then soak in cold water to wash off the starch
- ➢ Drain the potatoes
- ➢ Mix eggs, butter, milk, garlic powder, pepper and salt in a bowl
- ➢ Mix in the flour
- ➢ Add the shredded potatoes
- ➢ Heat your Air Fryer to a temperature of 390° F
- ➢ Add ¼ cup of potato pancake batter to the basket, cook for about 12 minutes until golden brown
- ➢ Serve and enjoy!

Nutrition Values (Per Serving)

- Calories: 255
- Carbohydrate: 42 g

- Protein: 7 g
- Fat: 8 g

The Classical Grilled Cheese

Serving: 1

Prep Time: 5 minutes

Cook Time: 7 minutes

<u>**Ingredients**</u>

- 2 slices bread
- 2 pieces cheese
- 2 teaspoon butter

<u>**How To**</u>

- ➤ Heat the Air Fryer to 350°F
- ➤ Butter each slice of bread
- ➤ Place a slice of cheese between the unbuttered sides of the bread slices
- ➤ Place them in your Air Fryer; cook them for 10 minutes, flipping them halfway through
- ➤ Enjoy!

<u>**Nutrition Values (Per Serving)**</u>

- Calories: 143
- Carbohydrate: 10g
- Protein: 6g
- Fat: 9g

The Ultimate Morning Spring Rolls

Serving: 4

Prep Time: 5 minutes

Cook Time: 5 minutes

Ingredients

For Filling

- 4 ounces of cooked shredded chicken breast
- 1 stalk thinly sliced celery
- 1 thinly sliced medium carrot
- ½ cup thinly sliced mushrooms
- ½ teaspoon of finely chopped ginger
- 1 teaspoon of sugar
- 1 teaspoon of chicken bouillon powder

For Spring Roll Wrappers

- 1 beaten egg
- 1 teaspoon of cornstarch
- 8 spring roll wrappers
- ½ teaspoon of vegetable oil

How To

- Prepare the filling. Mix the chicken in a bowl with the carrot, celery and mushrooms
- Stir in sugar, ginger and chicken
- Next, combine the egg with cornstarch and gently mix evenly to create a thick paste

- ➢ Place filling inside the spring roll wrappers and roll them up slowly
- ➢ Heat the Air Fryer to 390° F
- ➢ Using a brush, lightly coat the spring rolls with oil
- ➢ Place the rolls in the cooking basket and set it in the Air Fryer
- ➢ Cook for 3-4 minutes until golden brown
- ➢ Serve hot

Nutrition Values (Per Serving)

- Calories: 264
- Carbohydrate:42g
- Protein: 8g
- Fat: 5g

Chapter 2: Lunch Recipes

Everyone's Favorite Jerk Chicken

Serving: 6

Prep Time: 10 minutes

Cook Time: 20 minutes

Ingredients

- 48 ounces of chicken wings
- 2 tablespoons of olive oil
- 2 tablespoons of soy sauce
- 6 cloves of finely chopped garlic
- 1 piece of finely chopped habanero pepper with its seeds and ribs removed
- 1 tablespoon of allspice
- 1 tablespoon of cinnamon
- 1 tablespoon of cayenne pepper
- 1 tablespoon of white pepper
- 1 tablespoon of salt
- 2 tablespoons of brown sugar
- 1 tablespoon of finely chopped fresh thyme
- 1 tablespoon of freshly grated ginger
- 4 finely chopped scallions
- 5 tablespoons of lemon juice
- ½ a cup of wine vinegar

How To

- The first step for this is to take a large mixing bowl and pour in all of the ingredients to cover the chicken with marinade and seasoning

- ➢ Next, place the mixture into a 1 gallon re-sealable zip bag and put it inside the fridge
- ➢ Refrigerate for up to 2 hours to 24 hours, depending on your preference
- ➢ Pre-heat the Air Fryer to a temperature of 390 ° F
- ➢ Gently take the wings out of the bag and drain off all the excess liquid
- ➢ Take a paper towel and pat the wings to dry them off
- ➢ Place the wings into the Air Fryer cooking basket
- ➢ Set the timer to around 16-18 minutes and cook, making sure to shake the basket when the timer is at the halfway mark
- ➢ For more taste, serve the dish with ranch dressing or blue cheese sauce

Nutrition Values (Per Serving)

- Calories: 335
- Fat: 20g
- Dietary Fiber: 1g
- Protein: 31g

Perfectly Cooked Salmon With A Blend Of Dill Sauce

Serving: 4

Prep Time: 10 minutes

Cook Time: 20-25 minutes

Ingredients

For the preparation of the salmon, you will need:

- ➢ 4 pieces of salmon, 6 ounces each
- ➢ About 2 teaspoons of olive oil
- ➢ About 1 pinch of salt

For the preparation of the dill sauce you will need:

- ➢ ½ a cup of non-fat Greek yogurt
- ➢ About ½ a cup of sour cream
- ➢ About 1 pinch of salt
- ➢ About 2 tablespoons of finely chopped dill

How To

- ➢ First pre-heat your Air Fryer to a temperature of 270 ° F
- ➢ Drizzle each piece of salmon with just a teaspoon of olive oil
- ➢ Add some salt for added flavor
- ➢ Take out the cooking basket from the Air Fryer and place in the prepared salmon
- ➢ Let it cook for 20-23 minutes
- ➢ While the salmon is cooking, take another bowl and toss in the sour cream, yogurt, salt and chopped dill. This will be your dill sauce

➤ Once the salmon is cooked, top it with the sauce and garnish the final dish with a few pinches of chopped dill

Nutrition Values (Per Serving)

- Calories: 250
- Fat: 10g
- Dietary Fiber: 0g
- Protein: 27g

The Killer Skirt Steak To Die For

Serving: 6

Prep Time: 30 minutes

Cook Time: 8-10 minutes

Ingredients

> ➤ 16 ounces of skirt steak

The ingredients required for Chimichurri are:

- ➤ 1 cup of finely chopped parsley
- ➤ ¼ cup of finely chopped mint
- ➤ 2 tablespoons of finely chopped oregano
- ➤ 3 finely chopped garlic cloves
- ➤ 1 teaspoon of crushed red pepper
- ➤ 1 tablespoon of ground cumin
- ➤ 1 teaspoon of cayenne pepper
- ➤ 2 teaspoon of smoked paprika
- ➤ 1 teaspoon of salt
- ➤ ¼ teaspoon of black pepper
- ➤ ¾ cup of olive oil
- ➤ 3 tablespoons of red wine vinegar

How To

- ➤ First take a large sized mixing bowl and mix up all the ingredients that are listed for the Chimichurri
- ➤ Then take the steak and cut it into 2 pieces of 8 ounce sized portions
- ➤ Take a re-sealable bag and about 1/4 of a cup Chimichurri and place it into the bag. Put it in the fridge and let it freeze for about 2 to 24 hours

- ➤ When you want to cook, remove the bag from the fridge about 30 minutes before cooking
- ➤ Pre-heat the Air Fryer to a temperature of 390 ° F
- ➤ Take the steak out and pat in a towel to dry it
- ➤ Add the steak to the cooking basket and set the timer for 8-10 minutes if you are looking for a medium-rare steak
- ➤ Once it is done, garnish it with 2 tablespoons of Chimichurri and serve it hot

Nutrition Values (Per Serving)

- Fat: 600g
- Calories: 8488
- Dietary Fiber: 68g
- Protein: 168g

Yum Yum Honey Filled Pork

Serving: 3

Prep Time: 5 minutes

Cook Time: 16 minutes

Ingredients

- 1 pound pork ribs
- 1 teaspoon salt
- 1 teaspoon pepper
- 1 tablespoon sugar
- 1 teaspoon ginger juice
- 1 teaspoon five spice powder
- 1 tablespoon teriyaki sauce
- 1 tablespoon light soy sauce
- 1 garlic cloves, minced
- 2 tablespoons honey
- 1 tablespoon water
- 1 tablespoon tomato sauce

How To

- Marinate the pork ribs with pepper, salt, sugar, five spice powder, ginger juice and teriyaki sauce
- Let it marinate for at least 2 hours
- Heat the fryer to 350° F
- Place the pork ribs in your fryer and cook them for about 8 minutes
- In a mixing bowl, add soy sauce, honey, garlic, water and tomato sauce
- Mix well
- Stir fry the garlic with oil until fragrant
- Add the fried pork ribs and stir fry until fully coated with sauce

> ➤ Serve hot!

Nutrition Values (Per Serving)

- Calories: 297
- Carbohydrate: 10g
- Protein: 15g
- Fat: 22g

Authentic Korean Chicken Meal

Serving: 5

Prep Time: 5 minutes

Cook Time: 20 minutes

Ingredients

- 1 pound of chicken wings
- 8 ounces of flour
- 8 ounces of bread crumbs
- 3 beaten eggs
- 4 tablespoons canola oil
- Salt as needed
- Pepper as needed
- 2 teaspoons of sesame seeds
- 2 tablespoons of Korean red pepper paste
- 1 tablespoon of apple cider vinegar
- 1 tablespoon of hot water
- 2 tablespoons of honey
- 1 tablespoon of soy sauce

How To

- ➢ Gently separate the chicken wings into drumlets and winglets
- ➢ In a bowl, add salt, oil and pepper to the chicken
- ➢ Mix them well
- ➢ Heat the fryer to 350° F
- ➢ Coat the chicken with beaten eggs, flour and bread crumbs
- ➢ Place the chicken in your Air Fryer and lightly coat them with oil
- ➢ Cook them for about 15 minutes

- ➢ In a saucepan, add red pepper paste, water, apple cider vinegar, water, soy sauce and honey
- ➢ Mix them well and bring the mix to a boil
- ➢ Once the chicken is baked, place the chicken in the seasoning
- ➢ Coat the wings
- ➢ Garnish with sesame seeds and serve hot!

Nutrition Values (Per Serving)

- Calories: 809
- Carbohydrate: 54g
- Protein: 24g
- Fat: 55g

Macadamia Crusted Lamb Rack Roast

Serving: 4

Prep Time: 10 minutes

Cook Time: 30 minutes

Ingredients

- ➤ 1 garlic clove
- ➤ 1 tablespoon of olive oil
- ➤ 1 and ¼ pounds rack of lamb
- ➤ Pepper as required
- ➤ Salt as required

For macadamia crust

- ➤ 3 ounces unsalted macadamia nuts
- ➤ 1 tablespoon of breadcrumbs
- ➤ 1 tablespoon of freshly chopped rosemary
- ➤ 1 egg

How To

- ➤ First, chop up the garlic and mix it with the olive oil to create garlic oil
- ➤ Gently brush the lamb rack with the prepared oil
- ➤ Season it with pepper and salt as required
- ➤ Heat the Air Fryer to about 220° F
- ➤ Chop the macadamia nuts and toss them into a bowl
- ➤ Add the breadcrumbs and rosemary
- ➤ Whisk the egg in a separate bowl
- ➤ Dip the meat thoroughly into the egg mixture making sure that you drain off the excess egg

- ➢ Coat the whole lamb rack with the prepared macadamia crust
- ➢ Place the coated lamb rack in the Air Fryer basket, then slide it in the fryer
- ➢ Cook for 30 minutes
- ➢ After 30 minutes, slowly increase the temperature to about 390° F, and set the timer for 5 minutes
- ➢ Remove meat from the fryer and let it cool
- ➢ Cover the meat with aluminum foil and let it sit for 10 minutes prior to serving

Nutrition Values (Per Serving)

- Calories: 657
- Carbohydrate: 72g
- Protein: 26g
- Fat: 30g

Chapter 3: Dinner Recipes

Guilt Free Healthy Nuggets

Serving: 6

Prep Time: 10 minutes

Cook Time: 15-20 minutes

Ingredients

- 1 pound of minced chicken breast fillet (or ground chicken)
- 1 cup mashed potato
- 1 large sized egg
- Salt as needed
- Pepper as needed
- Olive oil spray

   Breading
- 2 beaten eggs
- 3/4 cup breadcrumbs
- Salt as needed
- Pepper as needed

How To

- ➢ Combine chicken, egg and mashed potato in a bowl
- ➢ Season the mix with pepper and salt
- ➢ Spoon out about 1 1/2 tablespoons of the mixture and form them into 1 inch bite sized portions
- ➢ Place the breadcrumbs in a bowl with pepper and salt
- ➢ Whisk an egg well in a separate bowl

- ➤ Dip the chicken and potato nuggets first in the egg mix and then in the breadcrumbs to coat
- ➤ Heat the fryer to 390° F
- ➤ Place the prepared potato nuggets in the cooking basket
- ➤ Spray with oil and cook for 15-20 minutes
- ➤ Serve hot when golden!

Nutrition Values (Per Serving)

- Calories: 225
- Carbohydrate: 21g
- Protein: 9g
- Fat: 12g

Finely Baked Asparagus and Potatoes With Cottage Cheese

Serving: 5

Prep Time: 10 minutes

Cook Time: 25 minutes

Ingredients

- ➢ 4 medium sized potatoes
- ➢ 1 bunch trimmed asparagus
- ➢ ¼ cup of low-fat fresh cream
- ➢ ¼ cup of cottage cheese
- ➢ 1 tablespoon of whole grain mustard

How To

- ➢ Heat the Air Fryer to 400° F
- ➢ Scrub and dry the potatoes
- ➢ Place the potatoes in the fryer. Let them cook for about 25 minutes
- ➢ While the potatoes cook, place the asparagus in a pot of salted boiling water. Boil for 3 minutes until they have softened
- ➢ Cool the potatoes and scoop out the inside
- ➢ Mix the potatoes with the cottage cheese, cream, asparagus and mustard
- ➢ Season them well and fill the potatoes with the mixture

Nutrition Values (Per Serving)

- • Calories: 293
- • Carbohydrate: 17g
- • Protein: 16g

- Fat: 18g

Very Mild Toasted Peppers

Serving: 4

Prep Time: 6 minutes

Cook Time: 15-30 minutes

Ingredients

- 1 medium sized red bell pepper cut into small pieces
- 1 medium sized yellow bell pepper cut into small pieces
- 1 medium sized green bell pepper cut into small pieces
- 3 tablespoons of balsamic vinegar
- 2 tablespoons of olive oil
- 1 tablespoon of minced garlic
- 1/2 teaspoon of dried basil
- 1/2 teaspoon of dried parsley
- Kosher salt as needed
- Pepper as needed

How To

- Add the diced bell peppers to a mixing bowl
- Add olive oil, balsamic vinegar, garlic, parsley and basil
- Add some kosher salt and pepper to season the mix
- Stir the mix well
- Cover and refrigerate for about 30 minutes
- Heat the Air Fryer to 390° F
- Place the marinated bell peppers in the basket
- Cook for 10-15 minutes
- Serve hot!

Nutrition Values (Per Serving)

- Calories: 148
- Carbohydrate: 17g
- Protein: 5g
- Fat: 7g

The Original Air Fried Butterbean Ratatouille

Serving: 4

Prep Time: 6 minutes

Cook Time: 35 minutes

Ingredients

- 4 of your favorite branded pork sausages

For the ratatouille you will need:

- 1 finely chopped pepper
- 2 finely diced courgettes
- 1 diced aubergine
- 1 medium sized diced red onion
- 1 tablespoon of olive oil
- Drained and rinsed 15 ounces of butter bean
- 1 15 ounce tin of chopped tomatoes
- 2 sprigs of fresh thyme
- 1 tablespoon of balsamic vinegar
- 2 minced garlic cloves
- 1 finely chopped red chili

How To

- ➢ The first step for this recipe is to pre-heat your Air Fryer to a temperature of 392 °F for about 3 minutes
- ➢ Take out the cooking basket and add in the pepper, aubergine, oil, onion, courgettes and let them roast in there for about 20 minutes
- ➢ Keep in mind that you are going to need to shake the pan while it is cooking

➢ Once done, remove the dish from the cooking basket and let it cool. Don't turn off the Air Fryer, just lower the temperature to 356 ° F

➢ In another saucepan, mix in the prepared vegetables with the ingredients for the ratatouille and simmer it

➢ Season it with salt and pepper

➢ Then take the sausages and put them inside the cooking basket of the Air Fryer and cook them for about 10-15 minutes, shaking them while cooking

➢ Take them out, and serve them hot!

Nutrition Values (Per Serving)

- Calories: 482
- Fat: 37g
- Dietary Fiber: 4g
- Protein: 17g

Fantastic Roasted Brussels and Pine Nuts

Serving: 6

Prep Time: 10 minutes

Cook Time: 35 minutes

Ingredients

- 15 ounces of Brussels sprouts
- 1 tablespoon of olive oil
- 1 and a 3/4 ounces of drained raisins
- Juice of 1 orange
- 1 and a 3/4 ounces toasted pine nuts

How To

- ➢ The first thing to do here is take a pot with boiling water and toss in the sprouts to boil them. Keep them there for about 4 minutes
- ➢ Pour in a generous amount of cold water, drain it and gently place it inside a freezer to cool it
- ➢ Take the raisins and soak them in orange juice for at least 20 minutes
- ➢ Pre-heat your Air Fryer to a temperature of 392 ° F
- ➢ Take a pan, pour in some oil and stir in the sprouts
- ➢ After that, take the sprouts and place them in the cooking basket of the Air Fryer and roast them for 15 minutes
- ➢ Finally, serve the sprouts tossed in the pine nuts, raisins and orange juice

Nutrition Values (Per Serving)

- Calories: 260.7

- Fat: 20.5g
- Dietary Fiber: 6.6g
- Protein: 7g

Delightful Chicken Escallops With A Crust Of Sage

Serving: 6

Prep Time: 5 minutes

Cook Time: 5 minutes

Ingredients

- 4 skinless chicken breasts
- 2 and a ½ ounces of panko breadcrumbs
- 1 ounce of grated parmesan
- 6 finely chopped sage leaves
- 1 and a ¾ ounces of plain flour
- 2 beaten eggs

How To

- ➢ Start by putting the chicken in some cling film and roughly beat it with a rolling pin until it is flattened to a ½ cm thickness
- ➢ Take another bowl and mix up the parmesan, breadcrumbs and sage
- ➢ Take the chicken pieces and dredge them in the seasoned flour
- ➢ After that, dip them in the egg
- ➢ Then dip them in the bread crumbs mixture making sure they are evenly covered
- ➢ Pre-heat the Air Fryer to a temperature of 392 ° F
- ➢ Take out the cooking basket, and gently spray the chicken with oil on both sides, then place two at a time in the basket
- ➢ After that, cook the chicken for about 4 minutes until they have attained a nice golden texture

➢ Once done, serve it with a generous portion of green salad

Nutrition Values (Per Serving)

- Calories: 573
- Fat: 26g
- Dietary Fiber: 0g
- Protein: 11g

Chapter 4: Snack Recipes

Extremely Simple Ham And Cheese Pin Wheels

Serving: 4

Prep Time: 30 minutes

Cook Time: 10 minutes

Ingredients

- 1 sheet of pre-rolled puff pastry
- 4 handful of grated Gruyere cheese
- 4 teaspoon of Dijon mustard
- 6-8 slices of Parma ham

How To

- ➢ The first thing to do here is place your pastry on a well floured surface
- ➢ Smear it with mustard and toss on the ham, making sure to sprinkle some cheese on top
- ➢ Gently roll up the pastry from the short edge
- ➢ Wrap up the pastry using cling film and place it inside your refrigerator for 30 minutes
- ➢ Preheat the Air Fryer to a temperature of 374 ° F
- ➢ Take out the Air Fryer basket and carefully line it with baking parchment
- ➢ Remove the pastry from the refrigerator, and slice it into 1cm rounds, then place them in the basket
- ➢ Slide the basket in, let them cook for 10 minutes until they have reached a nice golden texture

Nutrition Values (Per Serving)

- Calories: 404

- Protein: 16.4g
- Fat: 25.7g
- Dietary Fiber: 0.8g

Fine Vegetable Crisps With Nice Cheesy Pesto

Serving: 6

Prep Time: 10 minutes

Cook Time: 50 minutes

Ingredients

For the vegetable crisps you are going to need:

- 2 parsnips
- 2 beetroots
- 1 medium sized peeled sweet potato
- 1 tablespoon of olive oil
- ½ a teaspoon of chili powder

For the cheesy pesto twist you are going to need:

- 1 11 ounce pack of all butter puff pastry
- 1 tablespoon of flour
- About 1 and a ¾ ounces of cream cheese
- 4 tablespoons of pesto
- 1 beaten egg
- 1 and a ¾ ounces of grated parmesan cheese

How To

- ➢ The first step here is to pre-heat your Air Fryer to a temperature of 464 ° F
- ➢ Take a peeler and shave off super thin slices of the parsnips, sweet potato and beetroot
- ➢ Take out the Air Fryer cooking basket and toss the cut vegetables in the oil and mix them up with chili powder. Finally season them with pinches of salt and pepper

- ➢ Cook them in the Air Fryer until they have reached a golden brown texture (usually takes 20 minutes), keeping in mind that you are going to have to shake the basket from time to time
- ➢ For the cheesy pesto twists, roll up the pastry into a rectangular shape on a surface that is sprinkled with flour
- ➢ Keep in mind that the vertical side should be longer than the horizontal side
- ➢ Take a knife and cut the pastry in the middle
- ➢ On one half of the cut, spread the cream cheese and pesto then turn one half on top the other, creating a sort of sandwich
- ➢ Again, cut the pastry in the middle and create about 2 long rectangles. Then slice each of the rectangles into strips that are 1cm thick
- ➢ Gently twist each of the strips, pulling them in order to lengthen the shape
- ➢ Once the twists are ready, brush them with the beaten egg and spread on a generous amount of parmesan cheese
- ➢ Put them in the cooking basket and cook for 20-25 minutes until a golden brown texture has been achieved
- ➢ Serve either hot or cold depending on your preference

Nutrition Values (Per Serving)

- • Calories: 473
- • Fat: 23g
- • Dietary Fiber: 4.7g
- • Protein: 5g

Basic French Fries

Serving: 6

Prep Time: 5 minutes

Cook Time: 30 minutes

Ingredients

- About 6 medium sized peeled russel potatoes
- About 2 tablespoons of olive oil

How To

- ➢ The first step for this dish is to take the peeled potatoes and cut them finely into pieces of ¼ by 3 inches
- ➢ Toss the cut potatoes into water and soak them for at least 30 minutes
- ➢ Take them out from the bowl and place them on some paper towel to dry them
- ➢ Next, preheat the Air Fryer to 360 ° F
- ➢ Gently place all of the cut potatoes in a bowl and mix them up with olive oil making sure that they are coated evenly
- ➢ Place the potatoes into the cooking basket and place it in the Air Fryer
- ➢ Cook for about 30 minutes
- ➢ Shake the basket from time to time to make sure that all of the potatoes are being cooked properly

Nutrition Values (Per Serving)

- Calories: 473
- Fat: 23g

- Dietary Fiber: 4.7g
- Protein: 5g

Perfectly Cooked Potato Wedges

Serving: 6

Prep Time: 10 minutes

Cook Time: 20 minutes

Ingredients

- 750g large waxy potatoes
- 2 tablespoons of olive oil
- 2 teaspoons of smoked paprika
- 150ml low-fat Greek yoghurt
- 2 tablespoons of Sriracha hot chili sauce

How To

- First peel the potatoes and then cut them lengthwise into very thin wedges
- Soak the potatoes in water for about 30 minutes
- Take a dry towel and pat them dry after draining them
- Pre-heat the Air Fryer to a temperature of 180 ° F
- Before transferring the potatoes to the fryer basket, coat them thoroughly with oil and paprika
- Once done, transfer the potatoes to the frying basket and let them fry for 20 minutes. Make sure that you shake the basket from time to time
- After that is complete, take the wedges out of the fryer basket and place them in kitchen paper to make sure that they are oil free
- Before serving, sprinkle on some salt and serve them with a side of yoghurt and chili sauce

Nutrition Values (Per Serving)

- Calories: 123

- Fat: 2.2g
- Protein: 2.7g
- Dietary Fiber 2g

Healthy Zucchini Fries

Serving: 4

Prep Time: 10 minutes

Cook Time: 15-20 minutes

Ingredients

- 3 medium sized zucchini, sliced up into sticks
- 2 egg whites
- ½ a cup of seasoned breadcrumbs
- 2 tablespoon of grated Parmesan cheese
- Cooking spray
- ¼ teaspoon of garlic powder
- Salt as required
- Pepper as required

How To

- ➢ Pre heat the Air Fryer to a temperature of 425 ° F
- ➢ Take out the cooking tray and place a cooling rack inside the baking sheet. Evenly coat it with the cooking spray
- ➢ Take a small bowl and toss in the egg whites and beat them properly. Season with pepper and salt
- ➢ Take another bowl and toss in the garlic powder, cheese and breadcrumbs
- ➢ Take the zucchini sticks and dip them first into the egg and then into the breadcrumb mixture until the whole mixture adheres to the surface
- ➢ Place the prepared zucchini into the Air Fryer cooking tray and spray some more cooking spray on top of them

➢ Let them bake for around 15-20 minutes until a fine golden brown texture has appeared

➢ Serve them with marinara or ranch sauce for added flavor

Nutrition Values (Per Serving)

- Calories: 367
- Protein: 4g
- Fat: 28g
- Dietary Fiber: 3g

Amazingly Baked Apple

Serving: 8

Prep Time: 5 minutes

Cook Time: 10 minutes

Ingredients

- 4 apples
- ¾ ounce of butter
- 2 tablespoons of brown sugar
- 1 and ¾ ounces of fresh breadcrumbs
- 1 and a ½ ounces of mixed seeds
- Zest of 1 orange
- 1 teaspoon cinnamon

How To

- ➤ Firstly you are going to need to core the apples for this recipe by scoring the skin around the circumference using a sharp knife
- ➤ Take the cored apples and gently stuff them with all of the mixed ingredients
- ➤ Pre-heat your Air Fryer to a temperature of 356 ° F
- ➤ Take out the Air Fryer basket, place the processed apples inside and bake them for about 10 minutes
- ➤ Serve them hot

Nutrition Values (Per Serving)

- Calories: 53
- Fat: 0.4g
- Protein: 0.3g
- Dietary Fiber: 2.4g

Chapter 5: Dessert Recipes

Cute Miniature Apple Tarts

Serving: 5

Prep Time: 10 minutes

Cook Time: 8 minutes

Ingredients

- ½ cup plain four
- 2 tablespoons of butter
- 1 tablespoon of sugar
- Water
- 2 red apples
- 1 teaspoon of ground cinnamon
- 1 teaspoon of sugar

How To

- Heat the Air Fryer to 350 ° F
- For your pastry, add the butter and plain flour to a mixing bowl
- Cut the butter up into the flour
- Add sugar to the mix and combine
- Keep adding water until the whole mixture is evenly moist and can be made into a dough
- Knead the dough until it has a smooth texture
- Grease pastry tins with butter
- Roll out your pastry and line the pastry tins
- Peel and dice the apples and place them into the pastry
- Sprinkle with cinnamon and sugar
- Add another layer of pastry on top and make some markings with a fork

- ➢ Cook them for about 8 minutes
- ➢ Enjoy!

Nutrition Values (Per Serving)

- Calories: 316
- Carbohydrate: 44g
- Protein: 3g
- Fat: 15g

Astonishing Air Fryer Banana Split

Serving: 4

Prep Time: 10 minutes

Cook Time: 15 minutes

Ingredients

- 3 tablespoons of butter
- Bananas as required
- 3 egg whites
- ½ a cup of corn flour
- 3 tablespoons of cinnamon sugar
- 1 cup of Panko bread crumbs

How To

- Firstly, take a saucepan and melt the butter at a moderate temperature
- Add the bread crumbs into the molten butter and stir it for about 3-4 minutes
- When they have acquired a nice golden brown texture, remove them from the pan and place them in a bowl
- Take another bowl and beat in the eggs thoroughly
- Take another bowl and place in the flour
- Peel the bananas gently and slice them in two
- Roll the banana slices in the flour, followed by the eggs and finally the bread crumbs
- Once all of the bananas have been processed, take out the Air Fryer basket and place them inside
- Gently dust them with cinnamon sugar
- Let the bananas cook for about 10 minutes at a temperature of 280 ° F

> In the meantime, take a bowl and put in some scoops of vanilla, strawberry and chocolate ice cream
> Once the bananas are done, take them out of the fryer and gently place them beside the ice cream scoops
> Top it all off with nuts and whipped cream for decoration

Nutrition Values (Per Serving)

- Calories: 510
- Fat: 120g
- Protein: 71g
- Dietary Fiber: 92g

A Romantic Cheesecake

Serving: 4

Prep Time: 10 minutes

Cook Time: 15 minutes

Ingredients

- ➤ 3 tablespoons of corn starch
- ➤ 3 whole eggs
- ➤ 2 tablespoons of lemon zest
- ➤ 5 tablespoons of lemon juice
- ➤ 2 cups ricotta cheese
- ➤ ¾ cup sugar
- ➤ 2 teaspoons of vanilla extract

How To

- ➤ Mix together the sugar, ricotta and vanilla extract
- ➤ Add the lemon juice and lemon zest
- ➤ Stir everything until mixed well with a good consistency
- ➤ Heat the Air Fryer to 350° F
- ➤ Combine the eggs into the mixture one at a time
- ➤ Add in the corn starch and mix well
- ➤ Pour the mixture into the fryer basket
- ➤ Place the basket inside the Air Fryer and cook for about 35 minutes. When you hear the beeping, it should be ready!

Nutrition Values (Per Serving)

- • Calories: 392
- • Carbohydrate: 29g
- • Protein: 6g

- Fat: 26g

Soft and Succulent Egg Tarts

Serving: 5

Prep Time: 10 minutes

Cook Time: 10 minutes

Ingredients

- 1 bunch of spinach leaves
- 1 diced tomato
- 1 egg white
- Spray oil/ melted butter
- Salt
- Pepper

How To

- ➢ The first step here is to spray oil or brush the silicon mold cups with molten butter
- ➢ Throw in the spinach leaves and diced tomato, then coat them using the egg white
- ➢ Season with pepper and salt as required
- ➢ Place the dish in your Air Fryer cooking basket and let it cook for about 10 minutes at a temperature of 180 ° F
- ➢ Serve hot

Nutrition Values (Per Serving)

- Calories: 436
- Fat: 0g
- Protein: 0g
- Dietary Fiber: 0g

Surprisingly Eggless Semolina Cake

Serving: 6

Prep Time: 10 minutes

Cook Time: 25 minutes

Ingredients

- 2 and a half cups of fine semolina
- 1 cup of yogurt
- 1 cup of milk
- 1 cup of sugar
- ½ a cup of Tutty Fruity
- 1 and a ½ teaspoons of baking powder
- ½ teaspoon of baking soda
- ½ a cup of vegetable oil
- A pinch of salt

How To

- ➢ Take a bowl and mix in the yogurt, semolina, vegetable oil and milk
- ➢ Let it set for about 15 minutes which gives enough time for the semolina to ferment
- ➢ Make sure that the final consistency of the batter is similar to Idli. You may add some milk if required
- ➢ Once the semolina has been fermented, pour in the baking soda and baking powder
- ➢ Add the Tutty Fruity, gently cutting the batter into folds
- ➢ Take a baking pan and grease it with oil to make sure that the cake doesn't stick
- ➢ Pour the batter into the pan and tap it to ensure that it is smooth and even

- ➤ Preheat the Air Fryer to a temperature of 392 ° F
- ➤ Place the baking pan inside the Air Fryer and let it bake for 15 minutes at a temperature of 160 degrees
- ➤ Once the cake has turned brown, take a toothpick and poke the cake in the middle to check it has cooked properly
- ➤ Once done, turn off the power and let the cake stand for more 10 minutes
- ➤ Take it out and let it cool
- ➤ Cut the cake into small pieces and serve

Nutrition Values (Per Serving)

- • Calories: 117
- • Fat: 0.9g
- • Dietary Fiber: 0.9g
- • Protein: 2.5g

Jaw Dropping (OMG) Vanilla Soufflé!

Serving: 3

Prep Time: 10 minutes

Cook Time: 15 minutes

Ingredients

- ➢ 1/4 cup of all-purpose flour
- ➢ 1/4 cup of softened butter
- ➢ 1 whole cup of milk
- ➢ 1/4 cup of sugar
- ➢ 2 teaspoons of vanilla extract
- ➢ 1 whole vanilla bean
- ➢ 5 egg whites
- ➢ 4 egg yolks
- ➢ 1 ounce of sugar
- ➢ 1 teaspoon of cream of tartar

How To

- ➢ Mix the flour with the butter until they make a paste
- ➢ Take a saucepan and pour in the milk and sugar. Bring the mixture to a boil to properly dissolve them
- ➢ Add the vanilla bean to the boiling mixture
- ➢ Add the flour and butter
- ➢ With a whisk, beat the mixture until it is free from any lumps
- ➢ Simmer until the whole mixture reaches a thick consistency
- ➢ Discard the vanilla bean and set it in iced water for about 10 minutes

- ➢ While the mixture cools, coat six 3 ounce ramekins or soufflé dishes with butter
- ➢ Sprinkle sugar on the butter
- ➢ Take another bowl and add in the egg yolks along with the vanilla extract. Beat the mixture well
- ➢ In a separate bowl, combine the cream of tartar, egg whites and sugar. Beat until they have reached a medium stiff consistency
- ➢ After that, gently fold the egg whites into the soufflé base and pour into the prepared baking dishes. Smooth out the top.
- ➢ Heat the Air Fryer to 330 ° F
- ➢ Place the three soufflé dishes into the cooking basket and push the tray inside
- ➢ Set the timer for 14-16 minutes and let it cook
- ➢ When cooked, serve with powdered sugar sprinkled on top of the soufflé, and a side of chocolate sauce

Nutrition Values (Per Serving)

- Calories: 250
- Carbohydrate: 35g
- Protein: 8g
- Fat: 9g

Conclusion

I can't express how honored I am to think that you found my book interesting and informative enough to read it all through to the end.

The recipes in this book are only the tip of the iceberg and they were written to give you a glimpse of the true potential of your Air Fryer and what more can be done with it.

I thank you again for purchasing this book and I hope that you had as much fun reading it as I had writing it.

I bid you farewell and encourage you to move forward and find your true Air Frying spirit!

P.S: Dear reader! If you really liked this book, please help other readers to make the right choice! Leave your review about this book on Amazon. I will be very grateful to you! Thank you so much!

Click here to leave a review on Amazon.com